THE HOLE STORY
OF KIRBY THE SNEAK AND ARLO THE TRUE

AF073069

THE HOLE STORY
OF KIRBY THE SNEAK AND ARLO THE TRUE

BY

Greg Williamson

WITH ILLUSTRATIONS BY

Brian Bowes

First published in 2015 by

THE WAYWISER PRESS

Christmas Cottage, Church Enstone, Chipping Norton, Oxfordshire, OX7 4NN, UK
P.O. Box 6205, Baltimore, MD 21206, USA
http://waywiser-press.com

Editor-in-Chief
Philip Hoy

Senior American Editor
Joseph Harrison

Associate Editors
Dora Malech | Eric McHenry | V. Penelope Pelizzon | Clive Watkins | Greg Williamson

Copyright in the text © Greg Williamson, 2015

Copyright in the illustrations © Brian Bowes, 2015

The right of Greg Williamson to be identified as the author of this work
has been asserted by him in accordance with the Copyright, Designs and Patents Act of 1988

All rights reserved

A CIP catalogue record for this book is available from the British Library

ISBN 978-1-904130-83-3

Printed and bound by
T.J. International Ltd., Padstow, Cornwall, UK, PL28 8RW

FOR KIRBY AND ARLO, THEY KNOW WHO THEY ARE.

Kirby the Sneak and Arlo the True
Lived with the Burbles at house 42.

And Arlo the True, Arlo van Guard,
Watched over his everyday things in the yard,

His fir tree and fuzzball, his wetbowl and bone,
And Kismet the Catdog, who slept on a stone,

And out in the yard by a uniform mound
His cherished, cool, dug-up-down hole in the ground.

(He'd looked in his heart back when he was pup
And dug it a downhole instead of an up.)

He watched over everything just to be sure
That his wherearetheys all were still there where they were.

Now, Kirby the Sneak, Kirby Manchu,
Of a thousand disguises, unbeaten at *Clue*,

Dogma Cum Laude from Trickery U,
Kept a keen eye on said Arlo the True.

At the edge of the yard, past the reach of the law,
He drew on his drawpipe; he peered at his paw.

He drummed with his nails. He rocked in his chair.
He twisted his whiskers and stared into air.

And from under the brim of his sneaky slant hat
He schemed on the bowl and the bone and the cat.

What game could he play, what ruse could he do,
To bamboozle the scrupulous Arlo the True?

He could flip the bowl over to look like a lid
So Arlo would wonder what was it it hid.

He could bury the bone by the Burbles's brook
That sluices through shadows where sleuthhounds won't look.

He could stuff the ball into a knot in the oak
As Phase One of a bigger, more practical joke

That would take some straw, bungee cords, clipboard, a box,
And some UPS browns, with the Baden Powell socks.

⁂

But Arlo the True had a super good nose
That could sniff out the grade in your back-to-school clothes

Or the attars of blue when the summer wind blows
Or the red in a black-and-white sketch of a rose,

And Kirby the Sneak knew the True would discover
A bowl, ball, or bone under whatever cover.

So Kirby the Sneak tapped the brim of his hat
And took a hard look at Dame Kismet the Cat:

Like go bark in her face, make her hiss, maybe scat…,
But there were a couple of problems with that.

※

Kismet the Cat, Kismet the Wise,
Watched Kirby the Sneak through the slits in her eyes.

That crepuscular hunter, that somnolent purr,
That lightning strike wrapped up in quicksilver fur,

She could hear a slug slide and the sneeze of a snail.
She could make a cloud rain with the rings in her tail.

She could leap off a lamppost and land on her feet
And hear the small heart of a bumblebee beat.

She could fly through the night on the back of a broom
And see through pitch black in a windowless room

And foretell if a girl would say yes to a groom
Or if sailors were heading for fair skies or doom.

No, *Felix fantisimus*, Kismet Meow,
Could not be snuck up upon no matter how.

And for all his connivingest tables and charts,
His French curves and bar graphs and tactical arts

And schematics and plumb bobs and contour maps
Of the quadrant, a transit, and spring-loaded traps,

One other discouraging, serious flaw
In the plan which the Sneak almost instantly saw

Was that that that cat had a very sharp claw,
A very sharp claw on the end of her paw.

The sun had climbed high in the storybook sky.
The rindle ran wet, and the clouds were wrung dry.

The Dogface blonde butterfly silkscreened her skirt,
And earthyworms toiled in the Burbles's dirt.

The ants in East Antlia worked out a trade
To carry raw crumbs via bucket brigade

Through the grasshoppers' musical, country estates
With the mineral rights at near rock-bottom rates.

The hummingbird flashing a ruby bandanna
From the New Year's Eve blowout in Copacabana

Was zipping around like a sequined cigar
On invisible wings, having made it this far.

⁓

The golden-eyed sunflower shadowed the sun,
And the wren was rehearsing an old-timey run.

The frog in his wet suit, with scissor-lift legs,
Was diving the reef in the creek-bottom dregs,

With a laser-beam tongue and the ball-turret eyes
Of an air defense system for taking out flies.

The roses were crimped into decorative knots,
While at something like twelve aeronautical knots

The biplaneish dragonfly buzz bombed the top
Of the purple hibiscus with a boss turboprop.

The Better Boy boasted, the Early Girl blushed,
And the Signature Spider, unsquabashed, unsquushed,

Had written an invite (*RSVP*)
In her web to the moth, and the fly, and the bee.

So Citizen Arlo pulled out his list
And looked at the sundial he wore on his wrist

And flipped through his daybook to certify they
Were about where they ought to be this time of day:

The wetbowl and bone, the downhole and cat,
The ants and the spider and the rest of all that....

And Arlo Brown Dog rubbed the back of his neck
And ticked off the items, check check check check check.

He scratched his behindear and yawned a big yawn
And looked for a grassy green spot in the lawn.

He circled around it. He squinted. He sniffed.
Then he flopped himself down at the end of his shift.

⁐

But out in the garden the katydids trilled,
The trilliums waved and the woodpecker drilled,

And Kirby the Sneak stroked his long, sneaky chin
And blew a big bubble and soaked it all in.

The air grew more still. The hummingbird stopped.
The cat raised an eyebrow. The soap bubble popped.

And that's when it came to him, out of the blue,
A novel new way to trick Arlo the True;

He laughed in his dewclaw just thinking it through:
He'd *steal* the downhole. Then he'd *bury* it, too.

∽

So sneakily, skirtingly, circumferentially,
Cunningly, Kirby slunk, nay, provi*den*tially,

Over the ground where the downhole and mound
Had been stuck in the sun and were lying around

(A longwinded way of saying he crept)
While Arlo was dreaming of cheese as he slept.

He flashed the fourth wall a suave, Thomas Crown grin,
And then with his forepaws he filled the hole in.

～

But something out there seemed a little bit off:
You could almost have made out the hummingbird cough.

On the distant horizon, the earthworms homed in
On a talc, baby dust devil starting to spin.

The walking stick's foot inexplicably broke
Through the dome of a dewdrop way up in the oak.

The dragonfly sputtered, the ants hit a ditch,
And the Signature Spider, for once, dropped a stitch.

～

But Kirby the Sneak didn't see all of that,
Or the look of concern of Dame Kismet the Cat.

No, he cut his eyes north, and he peeked to the south,
And then he ran off with the hole in his mouth.

Now, Mr. McCornchowder lived right next door
To the Burbles's house in house 44.

He worked in his sleeves with a white pompadour
And overalls (blue) from the Barbary War.

He grew cabbage and carrots, chayote and chard
In the fertilized plot in the back of his yard.

He had a whole shed full of handcrafted hoes,
Custom-made rakes, and a watering hose

To fill up the pond for his gold-medal frogs.
But he didn't like holes. And he didn't like dogs.

And Kirby the Sneak slunk up to the shed
With the hole that he stole and the hat on his head

And his back to the wall by the composting pit
And a digital, seven-piece spymaster kit

Of lock picks, night goggles, invisible ink,
And a grappling hook if he needed to slink

Up the side of a freighter—but never mind that.
And never mind also that Kismet the Cat,

Like a magical leprechaun cat in a "poof"
Had materialized on the top of the roof

And was drowsily watching as Mr. McC
Stood trimming the leaves of the pin cherry tree.

O who out there knows if it's fortune or fate
That *later* comes hard on the heels of *of late*?

O who can distinguish *because of* from *after*
Or if it will engender disinterest or laughter?

Not even the vigilant, high-flying hawk
Can know something like that, or the Buddha-like rock,

Who can only see *now* and remember *back then*
And imagine how different things might could have been.

One thing about Kirby we *do* know was *when*:
He dug out the dirt, and he dropped the hole in.

∽

When Kirby took off, all you saw was a tail,
A blur in the wind, and a vapor-thin trail

That streaked through the stuck-open gate with a swoosh
And sucked the stuck-open gate shut with a woosh.

And Mr. McCornchowder brandished his shears
In a bowlegged polka with smoke in his ears.

∽

But Kirby was gone, gone back to his lair
In the Burbles's yard where he pulled up a chair,

A Dacron umbrella with fiberglass struts,
Iced table-leg tea, and pistachio nuts

To watch the hilarity sure to ensue
When they noticed the un-dug, smooth *not*-hole in lieu

Of the bound, hemispheric depression they knew
As The Hole in the Yard in the Land of the True.

Arlo woke up from his castles of cheese,
Slow-footed mailmen, squirrels in the trees,

And rolled-down car windows to stick his head out
Of on rides to the country with bugs in his snout,

But also the nagging dream vision he'd had
Of a black-and-white, rascally phantasm clad—

In the shape of a dog—in a hat and a tie,
That he saw with his extra-telepathy eye,

(Although whether his gift was more gut intuition
Or some sexier, out-of-this-world premonition

Like an incubus, astral projection, or wraith
Is a matter for science, dieticians, and faith)

Who was up to no good, Arlo saw right away,
Too theatrically aimless, too blithe or blasé,

Too dramatic in stopping and sticking his nose
Too approvingly into the Queen of Scots rose

With his paws crossed behind him, glancing around,
Pretending to whistle, toeing the ground,

And that something was fishy and probably wrong
Or it would be, or might could, before very long.

He whipped out his scratch pad and went down the list
Of all of the items that couldn't be missed

(While Kirby was giggling out of control)
When he came to the place where there wasn't a hole.

He searched in East Antlia, dragged the dazed brook,
And looked in the fir tree, and got the big book

On *Exploring the Rich Life of Holes* where he read
About canyons, deep space, the occasional head,

And historic, baronial socks, but the hole
That he needed—the one hole, the True hole, the sole

Lost at-large hole—to locate was, Arlo found fair
To say, null, in absentia, gone, and *not there*.

⁓

Kismet the Cat had beamed up to the top
Of the high-tech umbrella where Kirby the Fop

Took his tea in the shade with a tart, piquant zest
Of new tennis-shoe tongue to more savor the jest,

With a red gingham tablecloth, slices of lime,
And a handheld fan mister through Amazon Prime,

⁂

As Arlo Undaunted stepped up his patrol
Of the grounds and his wherearetheys *and* the lost hole

While not once losing sight of or scent of the trail
That sworn klepto took filching the Burbles's mail

And whom Arlo drove off every day of the week
With a menacing growl and a fearsome physique—

Except Sundays the perp was too yeller to show—
And a win streak like one or two thousand and O.

⁂

But the sun had begun to slide out of the sky.
The brook that ran off to the sea had run dry.

The earthyworms' dirts had turned hard as a rock,
And the dragonfly's motor was starting to knock.

The hummingbird noted the butterfly's gown
Seemed a little last season, a little run down.

The Antlian ants had abandoned their tasks
And put on small, antface-sized masquerade masks

To challenge each other at mumblety pegs
While the grasshoppers fiddled rye jigs on their legs.

The bullfrog, worn out from his scuba emprise,
Was unwillingly resting his Fabergé eyes.

And the Signature Spider, which just might be worse,
Had begun in her web, under some kind of curse,

A chaotic and homespun, untutored, unterse
But unvarnished, true eclogue in doggerel verse.

And Kirby the Sneak, even, Kirby the Crook,
Knew not to put something like *that* in a book.

But what could he do with stuff all out of whack?
When a voice like a catdog said, "Get the hole back."

Get the hole back, unh? Now, there was a plan.
If you needed a dog, well, the Sneak was your man.

So Kirby the Sneak reassembled his gear:
One snow axe, two snorkels, a hollow point spear,

A vanishing hand cream called U D'sappear,
One waterproof, undersea, eavesdropping "ear,"

Liquid spray smokescreen, Bath-B-Gone pills,
Two portable oil slicks, fake dollar bills,

An inflatable sandstorm, a ship-to-shore phone,
A genuine, black market, CIA bone

For stakeouts of henchmen and grifters and spies,
A reversible peephole, one Groucho disguise,

A hand-me-down astrolabe, stamps, odds and ends
Like *The BSA Guidebook to Bowlines and Bends,*

Two micro-stealth choppers with touch-screen control,
And a hole-poacher bag for the hole that he stole.

When he got to the gate, he could see he forgot
That the stuck-open gate had swung shut as he shot

Out of Mr. McCornchowder's gardening plot
When he dropped off the hole in the Land of the Not,

Regretting he didn't have videotape
Of his derring-done, brave, and heroic escape.

So Kirby, like Hannibal, paced up and down
With a scroll of the plans in his fist and a frown

Over last weekend's roundtable meeting of Mensas
On "Structural Weak Points in Privacy Fences."

And this one was long, yea high, painted green,
Like something right out of a fence magazine.

And that's when the cat said (remember the cat?),
"Dig a downhole on this side, and an uphole on that."

※

Well, that's what the cat said (with a catdog-like smirk),
And Kirby the Sneak thought, "By Jove, that might work."

So he pulled up his pantsfur and spit in his hands
And strapped on a headlamp with blue rubber bands

And checked the canary and took a big swig
Of couch-cushion Kool-Aid, and started to dig.

He dug like he'd entered the Treasure Chest Cup
All the way to the bottom. And then he dug up.

※

At the top of the uphole he got out the scope
From the Periscope Outlet to scope out the slope

Of Mr. McCornchowder's No Kirby's Land
For a booby trap, tripwire, or Big Dog Tree Stand.

The coast, as they say in the Coast Guard, was clear.
So Kirby the Sneak hauled up all his gear

And slipped on his No-Footprint HoleTracker™ Mocs
With an eye out for polar bears, cheetahs, and crocs

And sidled in silence alongside the side
Of the fence with the *Audubon Hole Hunter's Guide*

And a three-legged stool and a prospector's pick
And a Mercator map and a doodlebug stick.

And Kirby slunk back to the shade of the shed
With the lamp on his hat and the hole in his head

And the sack on his back and the map in his pit
And the pipe in his mouth and his hands full of spit

And Kismet the Quizzical Cat on the roof
In some kind of quantum mechanical proof

Of teleportation—but never mind that,
And never mind also the diamond point bat-

wing bowtie she was wearing was fine-tuned to pick
Out, by echolocation, the roar of a tick,

Or the crashing cascade in the wink of a bee,
Or the galloping hooves of the dwarf pygmy flea.

But Kirby the Sneak did not make a sound
As he hunkered down over the hole in the ground

On the three-legged stool with a come along winch
Hooked up to a tree and a canvas strap wrench,

A grease gun, a crowbar, a gator-back pole
And a folding screen sifter to sift out the hole.

⁍

It turned out it wasn't as hard as he thought,
And he didn't need *all* of the stuff that he brought.

He greased up the downhole, strapped on the wrench,
Stuck in the crowbar, cinched up the winch,

Tied off the tripod, punched in the pole,
And like Archimedes did popped out the hole,

As easy as pie, as easy as *cake*,
As easy as piecake piecake makers make,

And polished it off with a terrycloth rag
And dropped the whole thing in the hole-poacher bag.

⁍

And Kirby was cool. He was cucumber cool,
As he packed up the tripod, wrench, gun, bar, pole, stool,

And the sack full of hole, like a Santy Claus dog,
And canted his hat for the semi-long slog

To the Burbles's yard thinking, "Yessir, it's true,"
And patted his pockets and slicked down his -do

For the medals of valor he figured were due,
"You did it again, you old genius dog, you."

~

And that's when it happened, the way it'll do:
A shadow passed over, a mockingbird flew;

A leaf fell, a limb creaked, a galvanized pail
Swung in its well in an overgrown dale,

And Kirby the Genius Dog stepped on a twig,
A tiny, wee, little, small, not-at-all-big

Twig, the size of a splinter shaved off of a spoke
Of the Fairy's toy wagon Mercutio spoke

Of, its coachman a gnat, or the bit in the teeth
Of a Shetland-bred seahorse, or sword in the sheath

Of a Samurai elf, but a twig nonetheless,
And Kirby was in a, um, you got it, mess.

So what happened next, unh? I betcha can guess
If you've ever been in a um you got it mess.

The bowtie grew bigger and started to glow
With a radium green from the knot in its bow

And quickened a little and quivered to hear
The SETI-faint frequency tickle its ear.

The squirrel in the crow's nest on dogwatch detail,
Detecting the tell-tale signs of a tail,

Sent out the alarm in teeth-chattering Morse
To the rest of the treetop reconnaissance force,

Crying "Sneek Atak!" "Havok!" "Yikes!" "Ceece and Desist!"
And "Beware of the [very same] Dog!" whom the gist

Was in this case not lost on in spite of the well-
known but curious obstacle: squirrels can't spell.

―

The crow on his glide plane came out of the sun
To deride him in skywriting, "See Kirby run!"

The spigots popped up in a pillbox array
With the dogged, hydraulic intention to spray

Every inch of the feet in the yard they were in,
Including the inch that the Kirby was in.

And Mr. McCornchowder stood in his clothes
With one of his handmade, colonial hoes

And heard the Morse code and the clamor of crows
And was not fooled at all by the Groucho Marx nose,

But took a cold aim, and struck a hard pose,
And grinned with his mouth part—and turned on the hose.

⁀

Arlo was walking his usual beat
In the Burbles's yard in the afternoon heat,

With the baffling heist of the hole in his craw,
But doing his best to maintain common law,

When he heard the commotion of squirrels going nuts
And the squealing, retractable, landing gear struts

Of a crow banking south on its final approach
And the jeering wing beats of the jitterbug roach

And the sprinkler heads lock into place with a click
And wind up the waterworks *chhck   ch ch chck*

And then the faint sound of a dexterous wrist
Give a Craftsman brass nozzle a full quarter twist,

Then a spray and a scramble of paws and a yelp
That in the old patois of dogs can mean "help,"

Then the sound Arlo knew from just plain commonsense
Of a dog with a sack crashing into a fence

And crumpling up in a bundle o' paw
Like the bellows-like bendable thing in a straw.

⁓

The shock waves that traveled the length of the span
Were *one* sign of a glitch in Kirb's overall plan,

Notwithstanding his foresight, his intel, his wealth
In the engines and arts of deception and stealth.

Such birds as were left in the branches took wing,
And the hornets went looking for something to sting,

And the denizens, not knowing *what* had occurred,
Were on edge from the unexplained ruckus they heard,

And without even meaning to Arlo evinced
Real sympathy, *soul*, when he grimaced and winced

With his shoulders hunched up and his eyelids screwed tight
For this poor fellow-creature's calamitous plight,

Who, himself, by now sitting, was woozy and bruised,
As he nursed some loose teeth and a headache and mused

On the prospects of long-term emotional scars,
With a visible halo of songbirds and stars,

As it slowly came back what had happened, and how,
Which he, now that he thought of it, had to allow

Was a good illustration, from there on the grass,
Of the three laws of motion—velocity, mass,

Heat, inertia…, you know—having been in a state
Of straight, uniform motion until the closed gate

Intervened as the solid, immoveable source
Of an equal and markedly opposite force

That effected a very fast deceleration
In Kirby's forward progress, and soon the cessation

Of running at all, plus the lump on his head
From that change in momentum built up as he fled,

And the "*crash!*" that was some of the energy lost
When the paths of these two distinct entities crossed.

But after a while, from under the fence,
On the Burbles's side of these recent events,

The tip of a snout nosed up in a hole,
Like a berry aswim in a cereal bowl,

Circling around and sniffing the air
For whatever new perilous hazards were there.

Then up popped a head in a straw boater hat
With a carmine red hat band, while Kismet the Cat

On a weightless, invisible chaise floated by.
And Kirby Intrepid, Kirby the Sly,

Wet, kind of crumpled, a little bit hurt,
Tapped on his drawpipe to knock out the dirt.

~

The last song was over. The dance floor was swept.
The ants were asleep now. The grasshoppers wept.

The boy and the girl were engaged in a tiff
Over who should make up with the other—or if.

The hummingbird'd packed up his flip-flops and phone
For an early departure to Boca Raton.

The worms loaded steamers on old Model Ts
For the promise of vineyards and verdures of peas.

The bullfrog cut out toward the railroad track
With his lily pad rolled up and slung on his back.

The runway-slim butterfly, cousin to kings,
With quiet nobility, folded her wings—

Those kohl-shadowed profiles, those gold silhouettes—
And withdrew from the pageant. She sent her regrets.

The daredevil dragonfly, under the oak
With the shade tree mechanic, was fixing the choke.

And Arlo was down at the site of the brook,
Not doing much more now than taking a look.

Well, Kirby the Sneak sketched a few quick designs
Of breadthless zigzagging Euclidean "lines"

From point A (where he was) to a terminus Z
In the Burbles's yard (where he needed to be).

He wrung out his ascot and whisked off the grime
And synced up his fob watch to Greenwich Mean Time,

Then he hugged the pocked face of a make-believe wall
In a modified leopard-like Seal Team crawl,

Swung over the sandbox and slid by the swing
And clung to the least sunny side of the spring

Where the hornet nest hung like a bindle of fire
Or a hangar of organized, airborne, barbed wire.

With track-star technique, hinged at the knees,
Collecting his footsteps, at 20°,

He dove like a four-legged dolphin with fur—
And a fob and a soap bubble pipe, to be sure,

But in an exemplary dolphin-eesh *arc*—
Into a covert, sufficiently dark,

And ulterior blind to rehydrate and hide
(Redacted in Baedeker's *Most Secret Guide*

To Basements and Caves for the Fugitive Mole)
Under a bush by the badminton pole

With a stockpile of pitons, some ice skating blades,
Pro Matterhorn-class Edmund Hillary shades,

And also that wide open, welcoming view
The hardships and turns had maneuvered him to

Of the five-iron, fairway-green, walkable rise
Of a "second ascent" under tee-box-blue skies.

Who knows what he wanted: bright banners? acclaim
For all his mad skills? confetti and fame?

Or not to be heard from or looked for or seen?
The mere thought there was something to look for would mean

That no matter how good he was, studied or tough
Or ingenious he tried to be, wasn't enough.

But there Kirby was—not quite the North Pole
And with somewhat less buzz than he thought when he stole,

Carried, bagged, buried, ran, and re-stole
At grave risk to himself—on the verge of his goal,

Where at last, and at something akin to a stroll,
Kirby the Sneak *did returneth the hole*.

And almost at once, or at least pretty soon,
In the Burbles's yard on that clear afternoon,

The ant supervisor woke up from his nap
And yawned like a lion and opened the app

For places with coffee and all-day buffets
And straightened his slept-upon, shirt-collar stays.

The grasshoppers showered and started to hum
With comp wedges of grapefruit and Juicy Fruit gum.

The hummingbird put back his dive mask and fins
Into one of his Extra Small Rubbermaid bins

For a new (and "*hard!*") Cardio Mix at the gym
To hit those obliques for a mid-winter swim.

The butterfly, still—in this negligent age—
Seductive as ever, returned to the stage.

The dragonfly rockered some luminous toggles
And pulled on his World War I RAF goggles

In a bombardier jacket and flyboy chic cap
With a toothy thumbs-up as he waggled a flap.

The bullfrog reentered the airspace to smash
The facade of the creek with a coronet splash

In the targeted heart of concentrical rings
With a croak like the—*bo-ing!*—of door stopper springs.

The boy and the girl started getting along,
Though a little red-faced in admitting how wrong

They had been for the "Oh, just the silliest spat"
They'd forgotten what started, while Kismet the Cat

Was more like an aura or leftover purr
Of a theorized origin down by the fir.

And Arlo Straight Arrow, Cap'n Arlo, Brown Dog,
Went over the entries he kept in his log

To confirm with statistics his senses were sound
That the hole *had* been lost that seemed now to be found,

And measured the depth and diameter (twice)
Just to make doubly certain the math would suffice

To determine the volume and slope of the bowl
And resolve whether it was the bona fide hole

Or a bogus, imposter, fake, counterfeit hole
To replace the authentic one somebody stole,

And plotted it on a coordinate plane
To compare where it *lay* against where it had *lain*,

If "lain" can be said to be what it had done
Since a hole is an absence, a dearth of, a none,

And if "lost" can be said to be where it had been
Since there's nowhere an absence can *be* to be *in*.

But the latent leftover interior prints
And distinguishing tool marks were palpable hints

That it was and in fact the old hole on display
That he'd dug as a puppy dog back in the day

But that had in some fashion been taken away
And at length reinserted in just such a way

That only the eaglest eye could discern
There was something peculiar about its return,

*Al*most as if it'd been put in a sack,
Carried off, buried, un-dug, and put back.

⁐

Well, whatever suspicions old Arlo dog had
He kept to himself for the time being, glad

That *some* hole had turned up, if "turned up" is the word,
And convivial noises of mirth could be heard,

With the lawn bowtie green and the sky ribbon blue,
And doing the one job he knew how to do

As the Genius Loci, the *Watchdog*, whose view
Was that place on Earth behind house 42:

⌒

The walking-stick's waders, the teakettle wren,
The herringbone brook up and running again;

The earthworms, with faith the "rain follows the plow,"
Re-tilling the turf by the sweat of their brow;

The butterfly sunning herself between shows
In the very best treatment to date of "repose";

The hummingbird booking a timeshare for fall
At a breathtaking seaside resort with a mall

(And a fabulous Nordstrom's), fine dining, and art
At a cozy boutique, and *canard à la carte*;

The grasshoppers' barbershop *Songs from the Heart*;
And the dragonfly playfully strafing the part

In the buzz cut coiffure the hibiscus was sporting;
The boy and the girl and their (truly gross) courting;

The ants trading futures of sugar and wheat
On the mercantile end of East Antlia Street,

Like the Mesopotamians, long time ago,
With your chickpeas and myrrh and net capital flow;

Yea, all in pursuit, like the wetbowl and bone,
Of the teleological ends of their own

Individual natures and doing (by way
Of a visual nine-point inspection) ok;

And Mr. McCornchowder, up in his yard,
Just a-kickin' the dirt, but not really that hard.

In the pergola's arch where the Burbleses keep
Their Nomadic clematis that "walks in its sleep,"

The Signature Spider, unsquushed and restrung,
Had mended her web in the loom where it hung

From its halyards and cleats like a tiffany eye
To look at and frame stuff, you know, to *espy*,

Where she's the star pupil, who saw the whole thing,
Or parts of it, some, enough maybe to sing

Of two dogs and a downhole on lacework silk threads—
That is, when she's not sucking other bugs' heads—

So in more like a manner of speaking. But one
Thing she *did* do, and *should*'ve, when all's said and done,

Was to write down for everyone, stranger and friend,
Of the furtum, in cursive, succinctly, *"The End."*

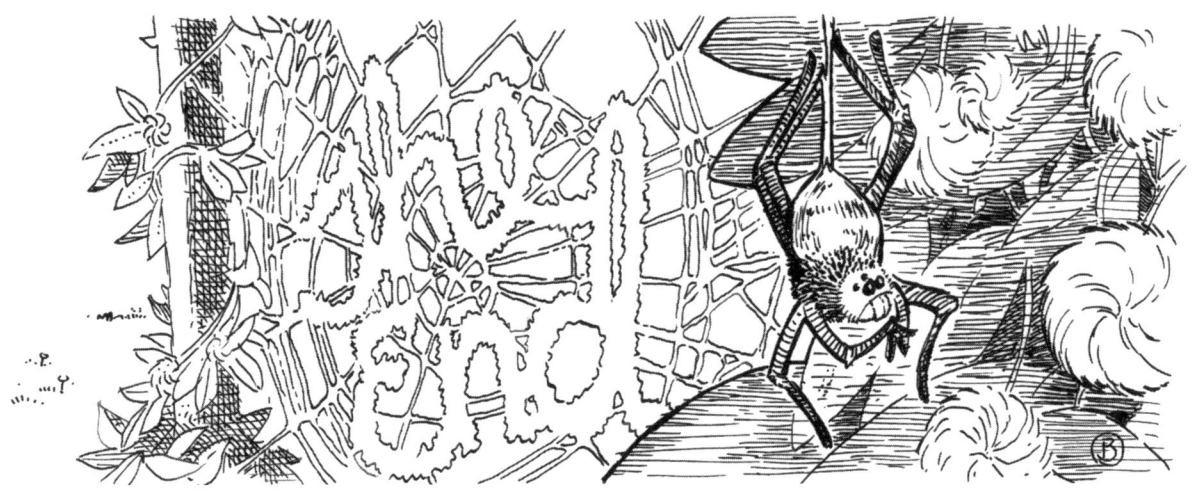

It's all in the books now. Or a bunch of it is.
And Kirby the Sneak, with a Jimmy Choo fizz,

Dropped his tools by the coat tree and slipped off his Mocs
And wrung out in a bucket his waterlogged socks

And dug out his specs and a taffeta chew
And a ladder-back chair with a pretty good view

From his den of the downhole and Arlo the True,
And a freshly packed pipe, and some thinking to do.

                                            ~

He looked out the window, or where one would be
If he actually had one, a pad on his knee,

On the balancing point of his equipoised chair
And watched the gold pollen spores drift on the air—

(To start a new life, he would venture, but where?).
He met Newton's Cradle's unwavering stare.

He tapped his right cheek with his right index claw,
His elbow at rest in the palm of his paw.

He took off the hat he was fond of to don.
He looked at it slowly. He put it back on.

He imparted a spin to the tabletop globe
Near the compass and square by his doctoral robe.

He held by two ends, evidently prehensile,
His American Natural #2 pencil,

Chewed like a corncob, in front of his chin,
Reflecting the depth of the thought he was in.

The downhole? Tough call. For all that's been shown
To be true about downholes, a lot is unknown.

If they're sort of at all like the Hawking's holes are
(While allowing for scale), calf-roping a star,

Well, then where is the rope? Who's making the throw?
If you heat the whole thing, does the hole shrink or grow?

When the hole "disappeared," did things feel a jolt?
Why'd the teenagers fight? Why'd the hummingbird bolt?

Why'd the earthworms pack up on a rumor of green
And the butterfly say *bonne soirée* to the Screen?

Released from the downhole's centripetal force,
Did they fly from or stay their original course?

                      ⁂

And Kirby the Sneak held his specs by the hinge,
With a tip in his teeth, and considered the fringe

Of the downhole's effects: Did they end at an edge—
As the yard in this case at the fence and the hedge—

Its dominion as fixed and defined as a dime,
Or smear like a ripple with distance and time?

                      ⁂

Or what if, instead, and intriguing the Sneak,
The hole, being empty, owed more to mystique,

Or belief in the hole, or to custom, routine,
(And possibly even without being seen)

Than it did to the felt, irrefutable sway
Of a kickable—what's the word?—*thing* you could weigh,

A totem of sorts that did nonetheless yield
The inversely proportional pull of a field,

The evincing of which, he surmised, would require
A little bit more than a bob on a wire

On the wind rose parquet in a Pantheon dome
(As at one time disheartened the bishops in Rome)?

⁐

Now Arlo was back at his usual post
With his Coke derby hat and a deputy ghost—

The even more steadfast and sure of the two—
From the lawless old west with the Pinkerton crew

Where the slow saloon doors swung and gunslingers drew
Of his great-great-great-great-great-great-granddaddy True,

With the patience of mesas and a coat of a hue
Of the riverbed sandstone the posses rode through,

And of whom legend holds he made even the worst
Desperadoes and crooks, the most feared and accursed,

Like Black Cherokee Bill and Bad Prairie Dog Dave,
Who would throw down with lightning and spit in its grave,

Start to quake in their kerchiefs and let the truth slip
With the flash of a fang in the curl of his lip.

And the old-timers tell he could wait out a rock,
That the rock'd give up. And it wasn't just talk:

He could stare a surrender sign out of a clock,
And he needed two shadows to go for a walk,

And he looked at this one big ol' barn door so long
That the paint just fell off. (And the roof tagged along.)

And you can still read, to this day, in *The Sun*
How he hopped on a train in the year '61

For the overnight shift to the Camden Street Station
To save Mr. Lincoln (and maybe a nation)

From the murder and knives of the Baltimore Plot
When the car with the True was as far as they got.

⁓

… And so Arlo the 21st century True,
With the Ghost True of folklore posterity knew

(If not in the flesh, or as plasma, or *seen,*
Then in *spirit*, at least, in that singular gene

He passed on to his pups and that keeps coming through
In the bearing and breeding that make them *All True*),

As the folk hero-dog's spittin' image and heir
To the deadpan, detached, imperturbable stare,

In the more or less middlemost part of the yard
By the hole he'd been given the privilege to guard,

Was re-aiming the rays of his weather-wise eye
In the calling he'd answered to scan the long sky

And the things in his province pursing their ends
And the four Cardinal Points and the Principal Winds

From the south corner stob to McCornchowder's gate
And to sit like a gnomon and *watch for* and *wait*

In the footsteps he'd followed (by fortune or fate?)
With a heart just as big as a country estate

And fidelity maybe his number one trait
And his back, flecked with sunbeam, hypotenuse straight.

⁐

Kirby'd been jotting some thoughts to himself
For the *Essay on Manners* he kept on the shelf,

With some diagrams, swirls, and a couple of quotes
He was privately proud of to add to his notes

For a series of lectures called *Get the Hole Back*,
How to Face Your Green Fence, and *When Sprinklers Attack*,

And the hole at the center of much of the din,
And how easily different things might could have been

By just plugging a few different variables in,
Or whether the box score was long written in-

to the stars when they very first started to spin.
Not even the rock, for whom peace is within,

Or the highest-flown hawk can know something like that.
And Kirby took off his worn, riverboat hat

And considered the last of his Jimmy Choo fizz
And the odds that of all the world's hats this was his.

⁂

He straightened the sideband and brushed off the crown
With a grin for those neon-lit nights on the town

And the days in the lab and the punts on the Cam
After sitting a particle physics exam

And the really tough spots or improbable scrapes
Or especially narrow, white-knuckle escapes

From some polar bears, say, or some saltwater crocs
Or some cheetahs or quicksand he had to outfox

With only his wits to rely on—and guile,
And the feet he was fast on, and Lassie-like smile,

And Scotland Yard compass, dehydrated ice,
A flying fish diving suit, pre-loaded dice,

Self-adhesive fake fingerprints, poison-frog darts,
A Viking-age sunstone with Coast Pilot Charts,

A collapsible, left-handed pole vault and pad,
A Highlander kilt in his Border-clan plaid,

Correspondence school Judo, raw courage, and pluck,
And an ascot for style—and the hat for good luck.

⁂

The shadows that earlier shrunk from the spot-
light, in witness protection or shy or too hot,

Were rotating clockwise at 15°,
Plus or minus, per hour—the fence posts, the trees,

The non-haint, opaque True, the umbrella, the gate—
And elongating, too, at a uniform rate

That involved their heights (A) and the tangent of theta
And from which you can generate tons of good data

With the circles' and triangles' intimate links,
As in Egypt gave Thales the height of the Sphinx,

A ship's distance from shore (plus some stars it could steer
By), and glimmers, in general, the earth is a sphere.

⁂

And Kirby reached up with his paw to his chest
For the railroad timepiece he kept in his vest,

In his signature neckwear and trademark chapeau,
And depressed the knurled knob of the crown in the bow

To unlatch the etched lid on the glass crystal face
Of his double half hunter gold pocket watch case,

Which he knew to be deftly, *exquisitely* filled—
From his time in the Worshipful Clockmakers Guild—

With the hole jewels and fine-tuned, contiguous gears
That ran (or kept pace with?) the minutes and years,

And inscribed *Cave canem*, as they used to display
In the foyer mosaics in Ancient Pompeii,

And properly known as an annular disc,
Like a plate with a porthole (to lessen the risk

To the skeleton hands in the face of the clock),
Or a torus or washer or bottomless wok,

Or a ring around Saturn—if you take away Saturn,
And quite a bit smaller—but, still, of a pattern,

Or the hole in the yard, or the circle and dot
Of the Circumpunct symbol, historically *fraught*

With tradition and meaning, like "End of the Line"
To The Boy Scouts, for instance, but also the sign

For Alchemical Gold, the Philosopher's Stone,
The Rose in its Cross, and the Sun on its Throne,

And, akin to the Pinkerton's unsleeping spy,
For the Masons and Templars the All Seeing Eye.

And Kirby the Sneak took a good look around
At the wetbowl and bone and the duplicate mound,

The hole he'd debouched from subjacent the fence
While the fate of the caper still hung in suspense,

The zeniths of salvos of crisscrossing streams
Still laying down fire in synchronized teams,

The hair-trigger hornet nest humming and hot
And just *itching* for someone to take the first shot,

The frog, double-chin blowing up like a bag,
With a top hat and cane singing *Michigan Rag*,

The butterfly bronzing, the worms in the field,
The ants readjusting their dividend yield,

The hummingbird's red, jacquard, scalloped cravat,
And the last-known location of Kismet the Cat,

And Arlo on point for the subtlest whiff,
With the chiseled, set jaw of a face on a cliff.

☙

And high in the Burbles's pergola's arc
Where the Nighthawk clematis steps out after dark,

In the oculus made by the arch at the top
And the half-circle gateway hung so as to crop

To a field of vision in ratio to pi
The seasons and antics of *time going by*

On the halcyon landscape it looked out across,
The Signature Spider hung down from the floss

In the hub of her spiral, symmetrical net
Like the traceried wheel of a window rosette.

☙

If there was a technical term like "tableau"
For this unrehearsed, silence-free, non-static show,

The Sneak didn't know it, but that's what he saw
Through the lens of the Jimmy Choo glass in his paw.

And he couldn't help thinking a couple things hinted
(If he scrunched up his forehead like lemons and squinted)

From way back to his coursework in Art for Beginners
At Diego Velazquez's painting *The Spinners*:

⁂

The folds in the fabrics draped over the stools;
Their distaff and noddy, his spymaster tools;

The Palladian arches in central relief;
The spider-as-artist-and-weaver motif;

Arachne as mortal and art as divine;
The ephemeral web as one more in the line

Of aesthetic succession from those most remote
And original forebears, rewoven by rote

And passed down with the blueprints and reengineered
As occasion allowed for and knack pioneered;

~

The hawk and the hummingbird likewise aloft
In the tapestried blue and the Burbles's croft

(Although minus the Marvin-the-Martian-hat fellow,
And no Bull and Europa, and also no cello,)

And Aerobie Pro Flying Rings up in the tree
Like the Ladies' two prototype Scrunchies-to-be

In a much-maligned future (and named for a poodle),
So if not, Kirby thought, the whole kit and caboodle,

Then enough of the boodle to notice a trace
Of a family resemblance in this time and place

To the masterpiece done with a paint brush and knife—
Except that was fiction, and not real life.

And Kirby thought, "Ah, maybe that is the word—
Real life—for this opera he witnessed and heard,

And thought it was funny, if just for a minute,
That to somebody else it would look like he's in it.

⁂

So if maybe not yet the most polished critique
For a scholar the order of Kirby the Sneak,

It could wait for a while. And he added that, too,
To such plans as he had for a tar baby clew,

A catnip-stuffed salmon, and hologram rat
For the purpose of capturing Kismet the Cat,

A freestanding, open car window and fan
With reusable bugs in an albacore can,

A dog house tricked out as a Buckminster dome
With no doors and a sofa of pre-chewed-up foam,

And a trophy for Flyball— a collie with wings—
To his burgeoning list of "To Think About" things:

⁓

Like how it could happen, or (would you say) *who*
Made the crucial advance in the spider worldview

Or jumped out of whatever career she was in
Into graphic design, saying, "I gotta *spin*!"?;

And which plays the more philosophical part
In the building of spider webs, nature or art,

(More the acorn its oak, or the swallow her nest?)
As the Lyceum Peripatetics professed?;

And the web as both fabric and visual aid
Of the threads and connections by which it got made:

A striving through eons in that cause celebre
Toward a dreamt, unattainable, paradigm web?

Or the know-how that's born of sheer countless webs spun—
And a family tradition—to get the job done?;

⁓

And Velasquez's painting's account of the fable
Of Ovid's Arachne's too honest, too *able*,

Subversive portrayal of Jupiter's tryst
(With deception—and jealousy, maybe—the gist)

Back in some even deeper, primordial mist—
Yes, this and the other things—went on the list;

⁓

Along with (and thinking, "Ah ha, that reminds
Me") his interest in archaeological finds

Of a general sort in his divers pursuits
Of the anthro- (and canine-) pogenical routes

Of his culture and bloodlines, and likewise their roots,
(Thus *successors* and *scions*, *departures* and *shoots*)

In the figures of speech that rely on and key
To the metaphors made of the *map* and the *tree*

And suggesting distinctions long since in debate
If a map implies *fortune* and tree stands for *fate*,

⁂

As over the years he had worked to compile
A pretty compendious Sneak Family file

(With the motto in mind, as he dug in the stacks,
Of Sir Richard Colt Hoare just to "stick to the facts")

That he gathered from seemingly fanciful tales
That turned out to be right in a lot of details,

And from passenger manifests, mug shots, mine deeds,
A few courtroom proceedings, a couple of leads

That he gleaned from *The Sheepdog Society Page*
Of the scandals and stars of The Golden Dog Age....

⁂

And whether it turns out the chart in his scrap-
book, in vellum and fixed by a coat-of-arms snap,

Is more helpfully *tree* or more credibly *map*,
It goes back to the '70's Great Wiston Cap,

The bluest of blue-bloods, the *legend*, who flew
To a win at The Worlds in a laugher—at *two*—

So precociously shrewd, hyperlexic, and fleet
That the losers made hymns to how bad they got beat;

⁑

And back further to 1901 and Old Kep,
Who was known as a kind dog, for sure, but his rep,

Beyond forty-five wins at the National Trials—
With contenders from all the Inhabited Isles—

Was the Eye of Compulsion, the Lunatic Eye
That cannot be resisted (and pointless to try)

The Eye of Unblinking, Surrenderless *Nerve*
That will stare down embarrassed tornados to swerve,

And that passed to his offspring, that's hardwired in
To the circuits of Kirby—and all of his kin;

～

And one father back further, one patriarch prior,
To ane Old Hemp of Cambo, the Foundation Sire—

From a silent and serious mom, and a dad,
Just a buy-you-a-fizz kinda guy at The Grad,

In whom *these* genes one time and forever assembled,
Who "worked so intensely he physically trembled,"

Who was "following sheep at the age of six weeks,"
"Introduced almost all modern herding techniques"

And flashed on the scene "as a meteor streaks"—
Of the Old World, original, Borderland Sneaks,

～

Grand champions all and great checkers of sheep
With their world-renowned monomaniacal creep—

And obsession with leaf rakes, Sudoku, and *Clue*,
And back counting paint in a seven-deck shoe—

And further back still, in the Sneak Family scrolls,
The unchronicled heroes on history's rolls,

Who themselves had to be, whether lucky or fitter,
A pup at one time in a mom-and-pop litter,

As Kirby conceived them, with rapturous yawns
And an abacus playing on glistering lawns

By the mountain-fed runnels and ice-water rills
Of the River Coquet in the Cheviot Hills

With their moorland horizons and rounded plateaux
And the glacier-gouged glens made an ice age ago,

And probably frolicking, probably biting
At skippers and falling, and probably fighting

In Yeavering Bell or on Bloodybush Edge,
Or chasing red squirrels in a hay meadow hedge

Or nipping the heels in the heather and gorse
Of the foals that grew into the Clydesdale horse

(With their bell-feathered feet—nearly twenty hands high
And as wide as a church—and intelligent eye

From one unnamed black stallion and chomping at birth
For the tug of the plowshare in breaking the earth)

And sallying forth through the bedstraws and thrifts
Without giving much thought to their myriad gifts

Or the infinite matters (of planning or chance?)
That evolved to the head-lowered, splay-legged stance,

Or *this* moment in time intersecting *this* heath;
Or the heirlooms of instinct they, too, would bequeath,

Like the penchant for herding and tireless work
From their ancestor wolves, and the head-cocking quirk

When they're given their mission—just playing and cute,
And incurring a couple of stings on the snoot,

And learning the Scottish for "Frisbee" and "ball"
In the picturesque ruins of Hadrian's Wall

In that phylum of barricades *not* part of myth
That he, too'd, had some recent experience with.

⁓

And Kirby Contemplative swirled in his lap
A fresh tumbler of fizz with an elegant strap—

To *garnir le cocktail*— he'd lately relieved
A Jane Birkin Bag of, in the sense of *bereaved*,

And imagined the long-running Walter Scott brooks
And the meadowland blooms he knew only from books

And the green, wooded valleys and faeries and rain
And the near-constant wind on the barren terrain

At the same pace precisely as centuries passed
And the rubble of towers and townships amassed

In the stony moraines and the burgeoning sprawl
Of the unhurried lichens, that lived through it all,

⁓

And in the long eye of the vigilant hawk,
But so quiet sometimes by a mirroring loch

You could hear the roused bee in the dew-misted cup
Of a rambling rose, or the sun coming up

On the faces of those loose, confederate bands
Of the families that roved The Debateable Lands

And his forefathers ran with through pixie-rich dells—
Like the Telfers and Turnbulls, the Burbles and Bells—

With their "lang spears and latches" on Turneyholm Trail,
Where they settled their quarrels, or Teviotdale,

Or at Frostylee just north of Bewcastle Waste—
Where a lot of the worst Steill Bonnets were based—

With their doublets and now-extinct Galloway Nags,
As adept in the fetlock-deep bogs as the crags,

And riding by moonlight the Kershop Burn Route
Into places like Tynedale for hijinks and loot

And maybe revenge with a secretive plan
Against maybe (who knows?) the McCornchowder clan,

And learning to hightail it out and abscond
Just before the Hot Trod's hue and cry could respond

Or the Warden catch wind of another bold theft
By the Borderland Reivers, who left us *bereft*;

˜

Or sporting by daylight and hanging around
With a jocular "foursome" enjoying a "round"

In a leisurely pastime that went by the name
Of the "golving" or "gouf" or the "Gentilman's Game"—

The first mention of which was its being forbidden
And its earliest artifacts found in a midden

Of "golving" clubs broken and smashed in a huff
Of beret-throwing rage at a ball in the rough,

But so pleasant Queen Mary is said to have "golved"
As her husband was murdered (that's still unresolved)—

And hiding the gouf balls or stealing the holes
That the golvers were aiming at under the poles.

˜

Kirby shook off a few drops with a tap
Of his forefinger claw on the Jane Birkin strap

With his head tilted back and his tongue sticking out
As he wondered what all of the fuss was about

With the Queen and her gouf game, her hunting and hawks,
And inventing the "caddie" for those spoiled walks;

And if one of the Sneaks might have spotted the Queen
Maybe reading the lie on a difficult green

Or taking a drop for another lost ball
And a dog cracking up at another close call;

⁓

Or if any of them could have filled in the blanks
With some names from among the anonymous ranks

Of those characters lost in the Scotch mist of time:
Like a prodigal uncle whose elegant climb

In Society circles—gold snuffbox, black tie—
Was the debonair front of a jewel thief or spy,

Or from Bannockburn dashing with word of a truce
After Edward was routed by Robert the Bruce,

Or drawing up plans with a compass and square
For Rosslyn Chapel with William St. Clair,

Or afore in the spray with the Templars' grand fleet
Making hard for Oak Island in feinting retreat,

Or your windblown, lone, capable Rover or Champ
Taking care of his flock, or notorious scamp,

∽

And if maybe that puckish, precursory crook
Could have helped with this clue in a history book—

Though a hundred and sixty-some years lay between
That last chronicled entry and Mary the Queen

Playing skins games for chokers with ladies-in-waiting
And embroidering pennants for bull- and bearbaiting—

That, in spite of some dubious spelling, implied
That the stories were true, and at least on one side

彡

He could trace back his lineage, long time ago,
To a "Collee the Doggee" in Chaucer's fabliau

(Or beast fable to others, or roman à clef,
Or mock-epic romance in the countrified hay,

And tour de force of authorial play,
Where it's hard to know *what* fruyt *who* means to display

Or how much the excursus is meant to convey)
Of a fox, or a cok and a hen, and a fray

In a ransackle barnyard, and wommen and dreams
In a famous buffet of post-modernist themes,

彡

In which Chaucer gives Chaucer's account of the tale
That's retold by the Priest of the Nun on the trail

Where a fox in the woods and some chickens at corn
Are pursuing "the ends for which sake they were born,"

And the question comes up, was it fortune or fate?
Was just *having* the vision already too late?

Could the rooster have outwitted fate if he'd tried?
Or *was* fate his inborn amnesia and pride?

Was it fortune or fate to escape it and gloat,
Since the fox had him caught by his *recheless* throat?

Or Reynard to let go, or the rooster to sing?
And which one kept Reynard from just eating the thing?

What would Collee have learned from the brawl in the yard?
Have a getaway plan. Be less dumb than Reynard,

(Though not totally lost on Kirb, drying his face,
Was how like to Reynard's was his own recent chase).

Would Collee have known, and with what apparatus,
To the instant, the time, like a strontium lattice,

Although even that pendulum swings in arrears
By a second or so over billions of years,

Or as Chaunticleer knew from dawn's peekaboo ray—
Be it training, his paycheck, his maize and métier,

Or a tic from his dad to a-doodle the day?
Like a cluck on the wall, Kirby let himself say.

Still, it's frequently useful to know, heading in,
Where you're standing, or sitting, or going—and when.

⁂

Kirby knelt by the safe, which had once been his dad's,
And, cracking his knuckles and licking his pads,

With the skill of a Peterman opened the lock
And extracted the timeless, Chaucerian "clock"

And first GPS system—the Astrolabe—(been
In the Scot family Sneak since "nobody knows when")

That's bequeathed when a pupil's deemed fit to admit
As an integral part of his schipherd dogg kit,

And holding it up to the afternoon sky
Took a few practice sightings with one open eye,

Then turning it over, still somewhat in awe,
Lightly burnished the bronze with the side of his paw.

∾

The Sneak shook his head, even now, at how smart
Was this brilliant achievement of science and art:

The capital letters and nicks on the rim
Of the body, or "mater," and known as the "limb,"

That divided the day, for exactness and ease,
Into hourly segments of 15°;

Interchangeable "tympans," or plates, that are matched
To the system of latitudes Ptolemy hatched,

With their stereographic projections of arcs,
The horizon, equator, and more, like the marks

For Crepuscular Sunset, the Zodiac's powers
As the *Houses of Heaven*, the Unequal Hours,

The Tropics, and right in the heart of the whole
Of the Firmament, *boom!*, the Celestial Pole;

⁂

And the "rete," itself, which is Latin for "net,"
That he learned as a pup, and its filigreed set

Of an artist's conceptions of dragons and Mars
And a dog's head surrounded by songbirds and stars—

The same stars that were shining (and pulling the strings?)
On Reivers and Emperors, Collies and Kings.

⁂

Why would Chaucer not simply have given the date
For the bird-hero's struggles (with fortune or fate?)

Unless his chronology's more of a spoof
Of a popular kind of sophistical "proof"

Of a paradox based on the nature of "when"
An inaction's considered to cease or begin,

Such that Chaunticleer could have escaped from Reynard,
In the *insolubilium* built by the bard,

On a handful of days in the April or May
Of a couple of years; or, perhaps, in this play

Of linguistics and logic, as much, Kirby thought
As, like, twenty-four hours *before* he got caught?

Time travel! Tempus Meander. Was that
The arrangement? Like Kismet the Cat,

Or what Kirby'd been working on? Maybe, but not
In those pop culture versions where somebody's shot

Via teleport, wormhole, or magical word
Through the fabric of time like a badminton bird,

As with Peabody's WayBack machine, though what irked
Him was that was all fiction, and his really worked,

Or it *will*, or it *will have*—it *might*—as he glanced
At the drawing board sketch of his new, more advanced,

Proto "DogGone" machine, re-encouraged in spite
Of some hurdles like gravity, matter, and light.

⸺

But before a garage-dog mechanic can climb
In a time machine, he's got to answer, *What's time?*

Is it made up of pieces, however minute,
Full of jiffies and trices? Or more like a chute

Full of water, a *river*, that leaves in its wake
Irretrievable pastness? Or more like a lake,

Be it wave-stitched or wrinkled, refulgent or clear,
With a boat ramp and swing, whereby *far off* or *near*

Is more spatial than temporal, all of it "here"
To go fishing in, ski across, watch from the pier?

Notwithstanding mixed metaphors (which, it is true,
About time's about mostly the best we can do),

Is it more like the debutante's ball, or the deb?
Or a wind in the jib of a dew-bejewelled web?

Does it flow over us, or do we flow through it?
(Is that even the question? Does it *flow*? Is it *it*?)

Is it more like the written-out score, or the song?
Can we ever re-right all the stuff we did wrong?

Does the "Arrow of Time" have a target? We know
It's flown by. It keeps flying. But who drew the bow?

So then was there a *was* there before that—a *then*?
Or a *where* for an archer to stand, or a *when*?

At what point did that state of inaction desist
And the heat lamp flash on, and the planets exist?

If the universe—*if*—is a lather-borne bubble
And way way way way past the lenses of Hubble

Are a googolplex more of them—you do the math—
In some cosmic Jacuzzi, well, who drew the bath?

But an urgent contingency Kirby still sought
To account for was, What if you're caught

In the DogGone machine when the universe stops?
What happens to time if the soap bubble pops?

But for now these reflections, these labors of love,
These inquiries he's a custodian of,

Could just wait for a while. For the moment what was
Was the Burbles's yard and the air were abuzz

With the zipper-seamed brook and an ice-cream quartet,
The dragonfly's prop and the hummingbird's jet,

The vaudevillian bullfrog, the head-turning flowers,
The workaday earthyworms putting in hours,

And the hornets, bees, wren, and a crow on the fly
In the general direction of *time going by*.

Kirby looked out through the porthole-like gate
Through the web where the spider was lying in wait

Like an X-marks-the-spot or the hairs in a scope
At the Burbles's ambling, emerald slope

And site of his exploits as modern day reiver
(For the same reason, maybe, the spider's a weaver)

And Arlo the Constant, the color of clay,
Who was still standing guard, without grievance or pay,

With the ghost of Great-granddaddy True at his side
As his benchmark for service and spiritual guide,

⁌

And pulled out the railroad watch from his vest—
With a paisley silk back and the Sneak Family crest—

Admiring the bench jeweler's arabesque case
With its dictum inscribed like a memory trace

Of a much older language, the genes in its roots
Still expressed in its progenies' hybridized fruits,

And admiring the practical hole in the lid
That revealed the clock workings solid lids hid—

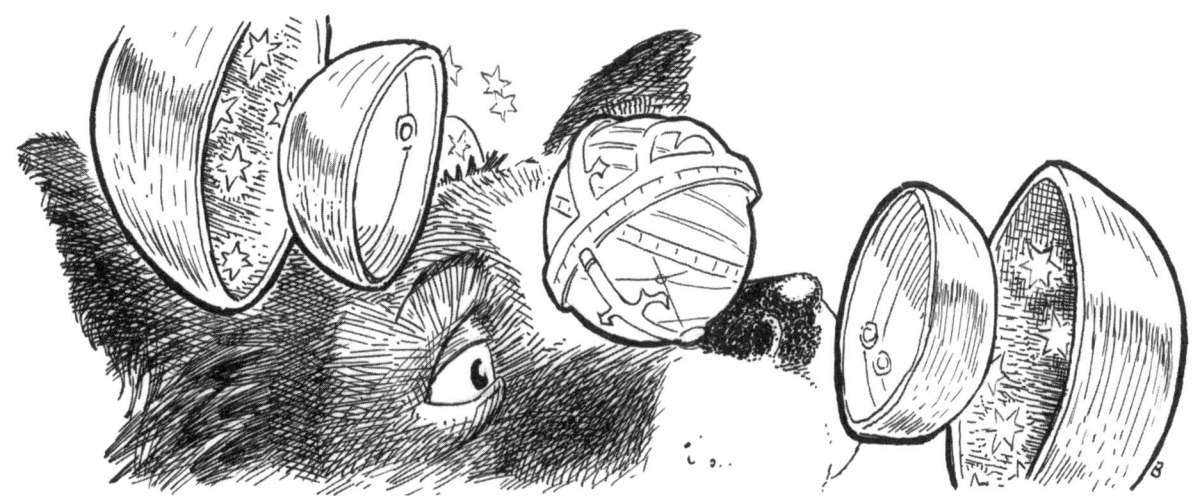

With its axles and wheels suggesting the notion,
To Kirby, of Ptolemy's theories of motion—

And that hung like a miniature rope tire swing,
If only in sharing a hole in a ring.

And he thought of the downhole, whose presence alone,
In its absence, created a centralized *zone*,

And the pivoting sprinklers the Sneak knew firsthand
Were to saturate sheepdogs in No Kirby's Land,

And the effortless, farsighted, high-flying hawk
Where he haloed high over the hub of the rock,

And the crater that dimpled the hummock of dew
Where the walking stick's foot was about to plunge through,

And Aerobie Pro Flying Rings next to his robe,
And the spindle that poked through both poles of the globe,

And the belly-flop bullfrog come splashing back down
In a princely, frog-toe-tipped, Doc Edgerton "crown,"

And those tympani ears that were stamped on his bean
Like chrysanthemum coins turning copper-tone green,

And the bucket that hung in the mouth of the well,
And the bee in the rose blossom's baffle-like bell…,

And still further examples for Kirby to find
Of the circles and dots of the Circumpunct kind:

Like the Scottish Rite ones that embellished his rings
And a lot of his other Freemasonry things—

The cuff links and tie tack, commemorative pen—
Of the Brotherhood's old, semi-secretive Den

So involved in designing the One Dollar Bill,
The U.S. Great Seal, and Capitol Hill,

And who over the centuries passed on the rites
Of those red cross, rich, white-mantled bankers slash knights,

Who uprooted to Scotland to restart the Lodge
When because of King Philip they got out of Dodge,

Where by Dodge they meant France, and thus took to the seas
With their fabulous wealth and the skeleton keys

To all kinds of arcana they found on the path
To the Temple of Solomon: masonry, math,

The Ark of the Covenant, Rennes le Chateau,
And a whole bunch of other things people don't know,

Like the Copiale Cipher, the Kennsington glyph,
And the Son-of-the-Widow named Hiram Abiff,

Or with charming naiveté quaintly pooh pooh
But that Kirby, himself, in fact, knew to be true

Of those refugee Templars, those pious, fierce monks,
Who arrived from the south with mysterious trunks

Full of relics and gold past the Isle of May
And a vow to avenge Monsieur Jacques de Molay:

⁓

Like that Midsummer Day, on the Feast of St. John,
Above Bannockburn Gorge, when some time after dawn

They emerged from the darkness and ghost-haunted fog
With their tunics well-cinched and a black-and-white dog—

The tactician/inventor and jack-of-all-trades
And advisor to Hugh in the Holy Crusades,

And exemplar to *even those* men of renown
Of a gumption and prowess that never backs down—

With the sound of a few chirping birds and the birr
Of the wind off the mountains that blew through his fur

And the snorts of the horses, some footfalls, the clink
Of their armor and cutlery high on the brink

As they crested the hilltop to mount an attack
With a mace in their hands and the sun at their back

Or aglint on their gauntlets, broadaxes, and swords,
Like the flash paparazzi at Emmy Awards,

On the huge English forces of Edward the Creep,
Whose noblesse and "great stature" were only skin deep,

That'd been caught in a trap where the disciplined Scots
Had bestrewn the wet field with caltrops and "pots,"

And just seeing the Templars were filled, to a man,
With such fear that, like Edward, they "panicked and ran."

⁓

And that was but one of the many good deeds
Of those knights who rode out on their sheet-covered steeds

In pursuit of disasters to strive to avert,
And bridge trolls to encounter, and always alert

For a lance to engage at a lady's behest
In an ever more gingerbread, mohawk-like crest,

Or a widow or serf who deserved some redress,
Or the bevvies of damsels in frequent distress,

And ferocious, occasional dragons to slay—
Though as far as the dragons went, Kirby would say,

As a longtime subscriber to *Science Today*,
They might not have been actual dragons, *per se*—

With their circular rondels, a coif of chain mail,
And for helmets a nosecone or upside-down pail,

And the patience and fortitude yet to prevail
In their ranging, perpetual quest for the Grail

That went all the way back to the Arthur of fable
And the often-remarked-upon shape of his table.

⁕

Ah yes, how it comes back around, Kirby thought,
In a circular fashion, the circle and dot,

And compelling enough, as a matter of fact,
That he'd drawn up some notes for a treatise or tract

Or a Stan Kaplan guide to an AP exam
On that polysemantic old ideogram:

(A.) The symbol for one of the elements (air),
(B.)The Brahmi for *Tha*, (C.) the Gothic for *Hwair*

(D.) a symbol for eye, or (E.) way in the sticks
In a couple of languages labial clicks.

⁓

But in any event—and in Classical Greek—
The theorist part of the pragmatist Sneak

Wasn't thinking about it in those kinds of ways—
And besides they were pretty well known nowadays—

But more, as Pythagoras did, in the sense
That the Monad, or circle and dot, represents

A (re)union of halves or a oneness that shares
The mutual flames of constituent pairs,

⁓

Or the way in which sometimes things interconnect
In what Kirby was calling The Downhole Effect,

Where a Great Central Vacuum, imagined or real,
Is the axis or hub of a notional wheel

Encompassing [question mark] [something] … closed set …
(He hadn't worked out all the details yet)

Maybe system of order… in which, in cahoots,
In etheric or, equally, earthly pursuits,

These soul mates, or natures, or complements join,
Or *coadunate,* like the flip sides of a coin,

Like the Yin and the Yang, in some versions of Tao,
As the Sneak understood it, the then and the now;

Like Watson and Crick, like the compass and square,
Like the helix and post of a circular stair.

⁐

Just what other examples the Sneak had in mind
Was a nut somewhat tougher to crack—so refined

Was the intellect, so cutting-edge, the new lexicon so demiurgic…, the cipher complex—

But about them, a lot of the wondering goes,
Was, like Newton, how much was right under his nose:

Like the bullfrog his bagpipe, the pendular swings,
And the two golden dogs in the butterfly's wings;

The earthyworms bound as they are to the soil;
The mechanic and dragonfly changing the oil;

The Spirograph seeds in the sunflower's swirl;
And fortune and fate; like the boy and the girl;

Like the grasshoppers' speakeasy psalms in the dark,
And the ants and their sprawling industrial park;

The hummingbird's annual trip to Cancun
With your clown fish and rays and a private lagoon;

The tomahawk woodpecker's cavitied tree;
The rose and the honey "it gives to the bee";

The hornets their halberds, the hole in the hive,
And the hapless next victim about to arrive;

And Mr. McC in his gardening clothes,
And the dog in the yard and a powerful hose;

And the shapes in the sun and the shadows they threw;
And the dulcimer wren and his mountain revue;

The clematis its trellis; the spider her loom;
And the lichen's bipartite, harmonious bloom;

※

Like Kismet the Cat's paranormal behavior as sometimes a particle, sometimes a wave,

Unconfined, it would seem, to our Natural Laws—
Not to mention the switchblades she kept in her paws—

Cruising around on a transporter beam;
Like the chaos of days and the alchemists' dream;

Yea, the wherearetheys all, in the lots that they drew,
With the genius within them to know what to do;

And one pretty good heist's unintentional(?) clue
In *The Case of the Downhole at House 42*;

With the lawn fairway green and the sky first-place blue;
And Kirby and Arlo, the Sneak and the True.

ACKNOWLEDGMENTS

My thanks to the editors of *AbleMuse* and *The New Criterion*, where excerpts of *The Hole Story* originally appeared. I am deeply grateful, too, for the help and encouragement of Philip Hoy, Mary Jo Salter, Joe Harrison, Michael Griffith, Brad Leithauser, Dan Ferrara, Jean Free, Leslie Harrison, Jay Moore, and Peter Travis, whose book, *Disseminal Chaucer,* Kirby read. A ginormous amount of gratitude goes to Brian Bowes for his brilliant inventions and collaborative expertise. And my love and biggest thanks to Emily Williamson for her patience and prodding and insight, who started the whole thing and should shoulder a bit of the blame.

A NOTE ABOUT THE AUTHOR

Greg Williamson grew up in Nashville, Tennessee and has degrees from Vanderbilt University, the University of Wisconsin, and Johns Hopkins University. He is the author of three volumes of poetry: *The Silent Partner, Errors in the Script,* and *A Most Marvelous Piece of Luck*. He has received an Academy Award in Literature from the American Academy of Arts and Letters, a Whiting Writers' Award, The Nicholas Roerich Prize, an NEA Grant in Poetry, and others. He teaches in The Writing Seminars at Johns Hopkins University.

www.gregwilliamsonbooks.com

A NOTE ABOUT THE ILLUSTRATOR

Brian Bowes received his Bachelor of Fine Arts in Illustration from the California College of Arts and Crafts in San Francisco, California. Currently he is enrolled in the Hartford University MFA in Illustration program and scheduled to graduate in 2016. He has illustrated numerous books, which can be found in bookstores and in university libraries around the world, as well as in the Rare Book and Special Collections Division of the United States Library of Congress.

www.BrianBowesIllustration.com

More Poetry from Waywiser

Al Alvarez, *New & Selected Poems*
Chris Andrews, *Lime Green Chair*
George Bradley, *A Few of Her Secrets*
Geoffrey Brock, *Voices Bright Flags*
Robert Conquest, *Blokelore & Blokesongs*
Robert Conquest, *Penultimata*
Morri Creech, *Field Knowledge*
Morri Creech, *The Sleep of Reason*
Peter Dale, *One Another*
Erica Dawson, *Big-Eyed Afraid*
B. H. Fairchild, *The Art of the Lathe*
David Ferry, *On This Side of the River: Selected Poems*
Jeffrey Harrison, *The Names of Things: New & Selected Poems*
Joseph Harrison, *Identity Theft*
Joseph Harrison, *Shakespeare's Horse*
Joseph Harrison, *Someone Else's Name*
Joseph Harrison, ed., *The Hecht Prize Anthology, 2005-2009*
Anthony Hecht, *Collected Later Poems*
Anthony Hecht, *The Darkness and the Light*
Carrie Jerrell, *After the Revival*
Stephen Kampa, *Bachelor Pad*
Rose Kelleher, *Bundle o' Tinder*
Mark Kraushaar, *The Uncertainty Principle*
Matthew Ladd, *The Book of Emblems*
Dora Malech, *Shore Ordered Ocean*
Eric McHenry, *Potscrubber Lullabies*

MORE POETRY FROM WAYWISER

Eric McHenry and Nicholas Garland, *Mommy Daddy Evan Sage*
Timothy Murphy, *Very Far North*
Ian Parks, *Shell Island*
V. Penelope Pelizzon, *Whose Flesh is Flame, Whose Bone is Time*
Chris Preddle, *Cattle Console Him*
Shelley Puhak, *Guinevere in Baltimore*
Christopher Ricks, ed., *Joining Music with Reason: 34 Poets, British and American, Oxford 2004-2009*
Daniel Rifenburgh, *Advent*
Mary Jo Salter, *It's Hard to Say: Selected Poems*
W. D. Snodgrass, *Not for Specialists: New & Selected Poems*
Mark Strand, *Almost Invisible*
Mark Strand, *Blizzard of One*
Bradford Gray Telford, *Perfect Hurt*
Matthew Thorburn, *This Time Tomorrow*
Cody Walker, *Shuffle and Breakdown*
Deborah Warren, *The Size of Happiness*
Clive Watkins, *Already the Flames*
Clive Watkins, *Jigsaw*
Richard Wilbur, *Anterooms*
Richard Wilbur, *Mayflies*
Richard Wilbur, *Collected Poems 1943-2004*
Norman Williams, *One Unblinking Eye*
Greg Williamson, *A Most Marvelous Piece of Luck*